# World of Wonder
# Minibeasts

Written by Danielle Stevens

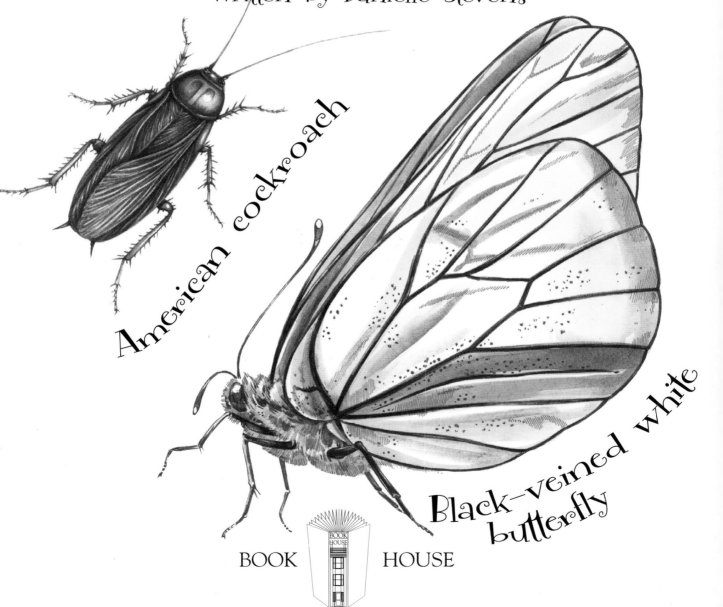

American cockroach

Black-veined white butterfly

BOOK HOUSE

# Contents

# What are minibeasts?

**M**inibeasts are the billions of **insects**, spiders and other creepy-crawlies that live all around the world. Scientists know about more than one million types, or **species**, of minibeast.

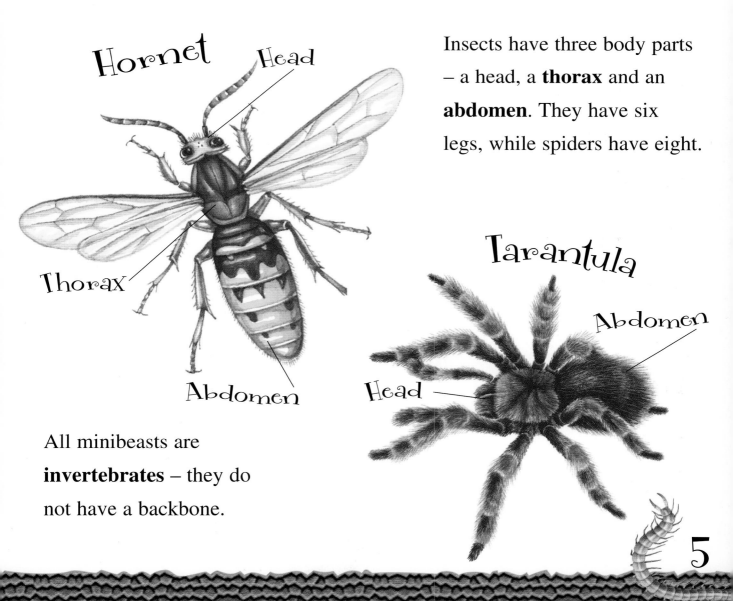

Hornet

Head

Thorax

Abdomen

Insects have three body parts – a head, a **thorax** and an **abdomen**. They have six legs, while spiders have eight.

Tarantula

Abdomen

Head

All minibeasts are **invertebrates** – they do not have a backbone.

5

# Can minibeasts build big homes?

**Social insects** like termites, bees and ants work together to build big nests where they live in hundreds of thousands. By living together in large numbers, social insects protect one another from **predators**.

## True or False?
Weaver ants use silk to build their nest.

Answers on page 31

Termite mound

Termite mounds can be huge – up to 13 metres high and 30 metres round.

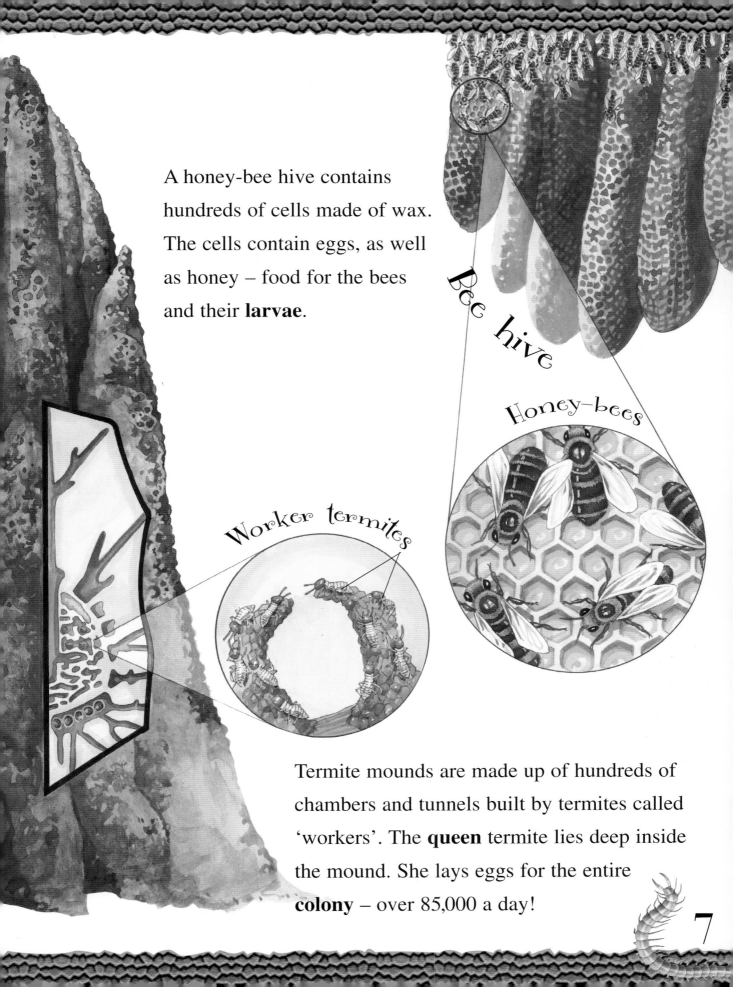

A honey-bee hive contains hundreds of cells made of wax. The cells contain eggs, as well as honey – food for the bees and their **larvae**.

Bee hive

Honey-bees

Worker termites

Termite mounds are made up of hundreds of chambers and tunnels built by termites called 'workers'. The **queen** termite lies deep inside the mound. She lays eggs for the entire **colony** – over 85,000 a day!

# Which insects use disguises?

**M**any species of insect use disguises or **camouflage** to hide from predators – and **prey**.

Stick insect

Is there a stick insect hiding among the green plants?

The beautiful orchid mantis looks just like the flower it lives on. Can you see its pink body?

Orchid mantis

## True or False?
Praying mantises hunt frogs and rodents.

? ? ? ? ?

Answers on page 31

A leaf insect has a body and legs shaped like leaves. It even has 'leaves' that look as though they've been chewed by other insects!

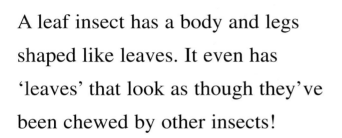

Leaf insect

'Chewed' edge

Lappet moths have patterned wings. Can you see one among the autumn leaves?

Lappet moth

Praying mantis

Praying mantises use their leafy disguises to sneak up on prey, and then pounce with their two front limbs.

# Can minibeasts cause problems?

$S$ome beetles can cause problems for people by chewing through wood, paper and even electrical wire. Desert locusts also cause big problems by eating large amounts of crops.

## Colorado potato beetle

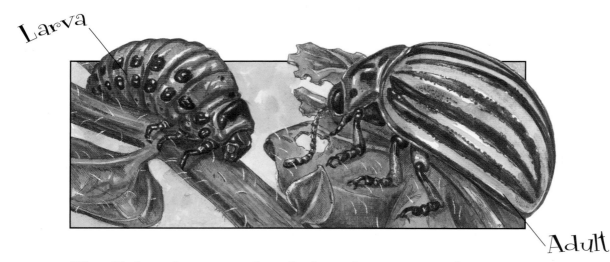

Larva

Adult

The Colorado potato beetle lays its eggs on the underside of potato plant leaves. When the eggs hatch, the larvae (young) eat the plant. They can destroy entire potato crops.

Wood-boring beetles (right) bury their eggs inside wood. When they hatch, the larvae weaken the wood by eating it from the inside.

Longhorn beetle

Deathwatch beetle

Flathead borer

## Desert locusts

Desert locusts form **swarms** of up to 40 million and can eat through up to 80,000 tonnes of food a day. In 1954, a swarm of 5 billion locusts flew across Africa, destroying tonnes of crops.

# Which minibeasts are parasites?

**M**inibeasts such as fleas are **parasites** – they live or feed on the bodies of other animals. Some parasites bite humans. They irritate our skin and can spread diseases.

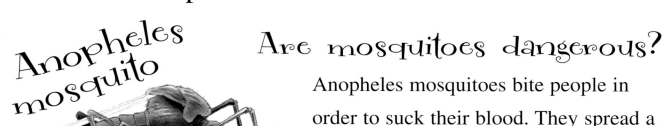

Anopheles mosquito

## Are mosquitoes dangerous?

Anopheles mosquitoes bite people in order to suck their blood. They spread a deadly disease called malaria which affects 100 million people a year.

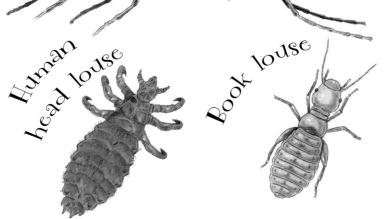

Human head louse

Book louse

Bedbug

Head louse bites make their victims' heads itch.

Book lice eat and destroy old books and paper.

Bedbugs live on blood. They like to live in people's homes.

# Black rat

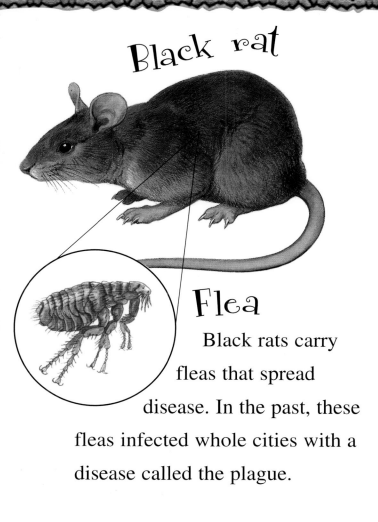

## Flea

Black rats carry fleas that spread disease. In the past, these fleas infected whole cities with a disease called the plague.

## True or False?

Mosquito larvae breathe through snorkels.

Answers on page 31

The dog flea can jump an incredible 30 cm. It doesn't sound like much, but that's the equivalent of a human jumping the length of a football pitch!

## Assassin bug

## Deer tick

## Dog flea

This blood-sucking bug lies in wait before ambushing its prey.

Ticks feed by plunging their whole head into an animal's body.

13

# Why are butterflies so colourful?

Butterflies have large, coloured wings that attract mates and scare off predators. Some butterflies are poisonous to other animals. Their colourful markings act as a warning to birds and lizards who might mistake them for a tasty meal.

## True or False?

Butterflies are born with wings.

? ? ? ?

Answers on page 31

Rippon's birdwing

The wings of a butterfly are symmetrical – they are a mirror image of each other.

**Flutter**

Swallowtail

Like all butterflies, swallowtails have long, curly tongues, which can be unfolded to drink the **nectar** inside flowers.

Paradise birdwing

There are over 600 species of swallowtail butterfly. The giant African swallowtail is the largest butterfly in Africa.

Paradise birdwing butterflies live in the forests of Papua New Guinea and are thought to be very rare.

# Can crickets sing?

A cricket doesn't have a voice, but it can 'sing' using its wings. Male crickets rub their wings together to make a 'chirrup' sound. This attracts a female, who will follow the noise.

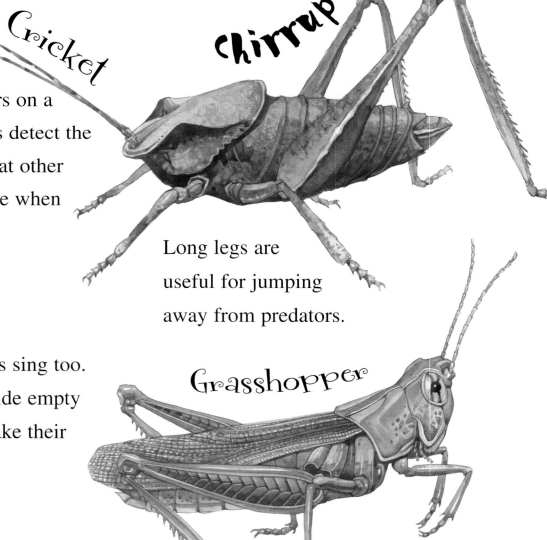

Cricket

Chirrup

Grasshopper

The tiny hairs on a cricket's legs detect the vibrations that other crickets make when they sing.

Long legs are useful for jumping away from predators.

Grasshoppers sing too. Some sit inside empty bottles to make their song louder.

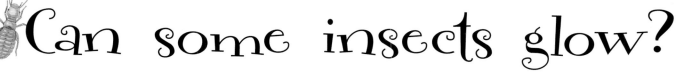

# Can some insects glow?

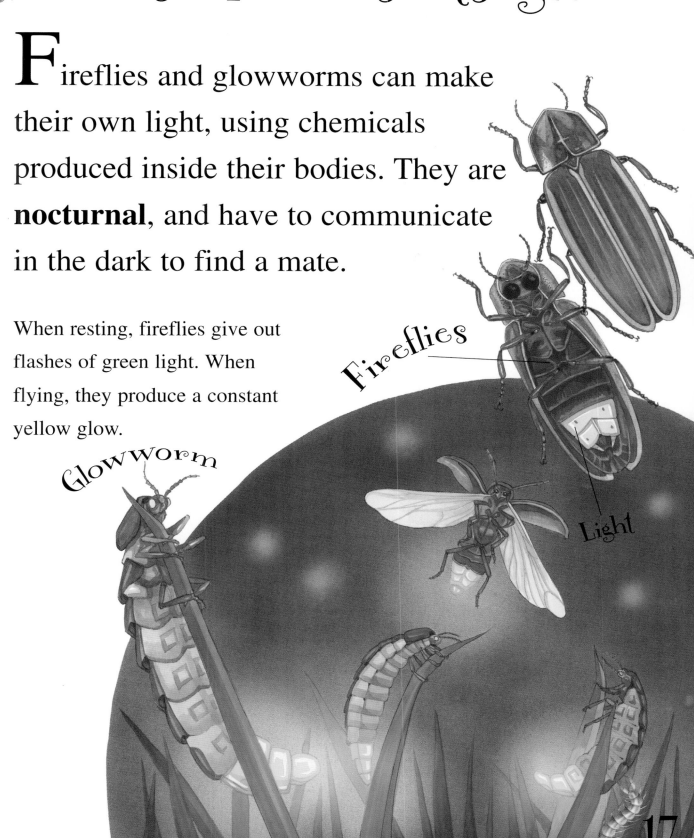

Fireflies and glowworms can make their own light, using chemicals produced inside their bodies. They are **nocturnal**, and have to communicate in the dark to find a mate.

When resting, fireflies give out flashes of green light. When flying, they produce a constant yellow glow.

Glowworm

Fireflies

Light

17

# How many legs do millipedes have?

**M**illipedes and centipedes are not insects. How can you tell? They have a lot more than six legs! Millipedes have up to 750 legs. Centipedes have 30–354, depending on the species.

Millipede

Segments

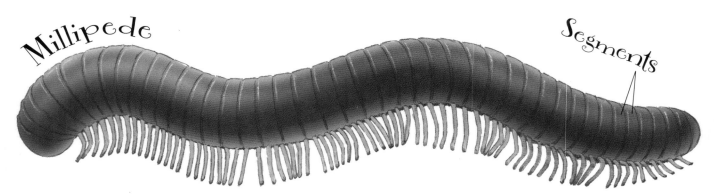

## True or False?
Millipedes curl up when attacked.

Answers on page 31

The bodies of millipedes and centipedes are divided into segments. Millipedes have two pairs of legs on each segment. Centipedes have one pair of legs on each segment.

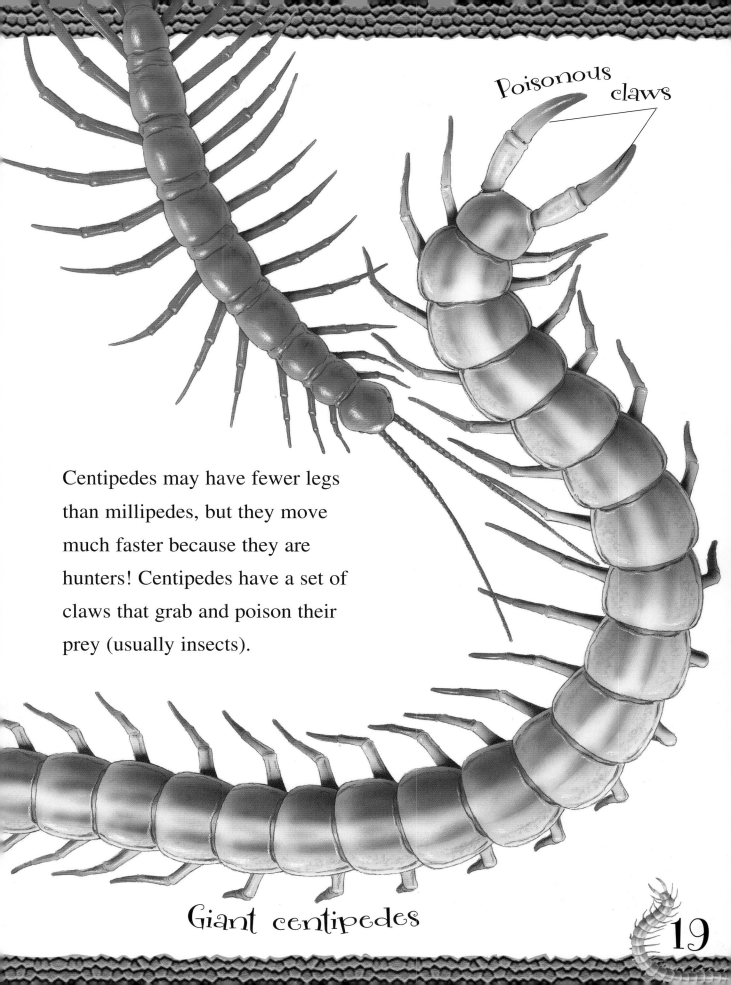

Poisonous claws

Centipedes may have fewer legs than millipedes, but they move much faster because they are hunters! Centipedes have a set of claws that grab and poison their prey (usually insects).

Giant centipedes

19

# What's inside a wasps' nest?

Inside a wasps' nest live the queen wasp, worker wasps, eggs and larvae. The nest grows in size as more wasps are born.

Wasps build their nest using a paste that they make by chewing up dead wood. This paste dries to form the paper-like walls of a nest.

Chewing wood

Cross-section of a nest

Wasps are aggressive animals that will attack and sting anything that threatens their nest. Unlike bees, they can sting over and over again without dying.

Buzz

Wasp

Sting

# Do ants work together?

Like termites, ants are social insects that live in colonies of many thousands. Most colonies are very organised – every ant has a job to do. Some are worker ants that collect food. Others are soldiers, who protect the nest.

Amazon ants are not just soldiers – they are kidnappers, too! Amazon ants will raid another ant nest and steal its eggs and larvae. When the kidnapped young grow into adults, they become workers for the Amazon ants.

Amazon ant

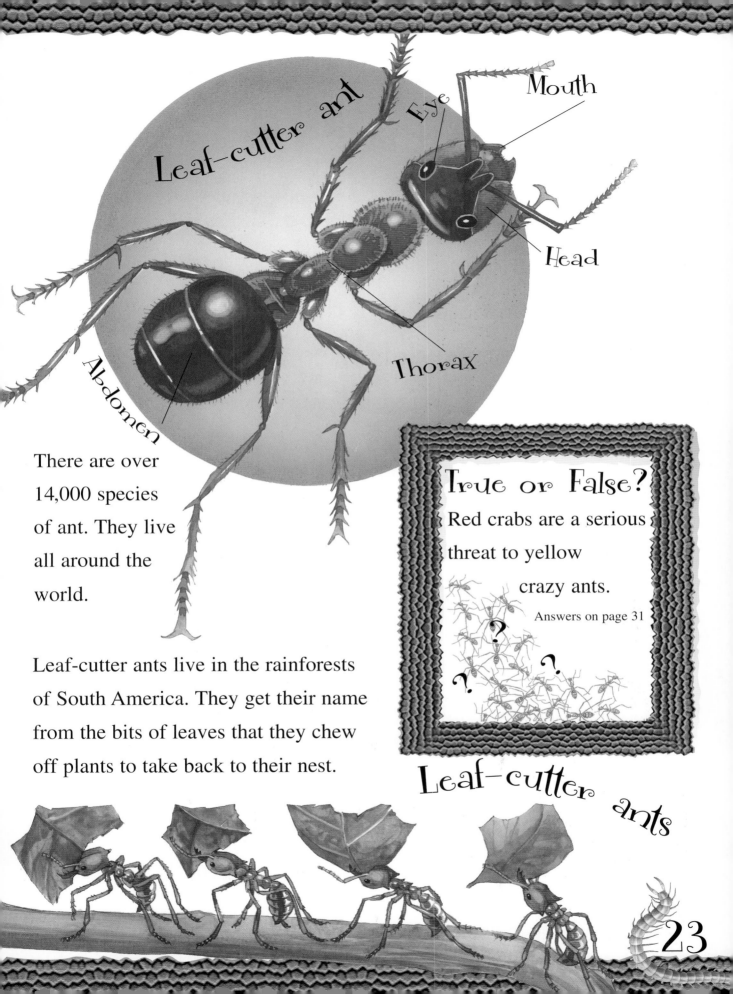

Leaf-cutter ant

Eye

Mouth

Head

Thorax

Abdomen

There are over 14,000 species of ant. They live all around the world.

Leaf-cutter ants live in the rainforests of South America. They get their name from the bits of leaves that they chew off plants to take back to their nest.

## True or False?

Red crabs are a serious threat to yellow crazy ants.

Answers on page 31

Leaf-cutter ants

23

# How do spiders have babies?

Spiders start life inside an egg. Spider mothers lay hundreds of eggs at a time. The baby spiders (or spiderlings) all hatch together. Each spiderling makes a tiny silk parachute and is carried away by the wind.

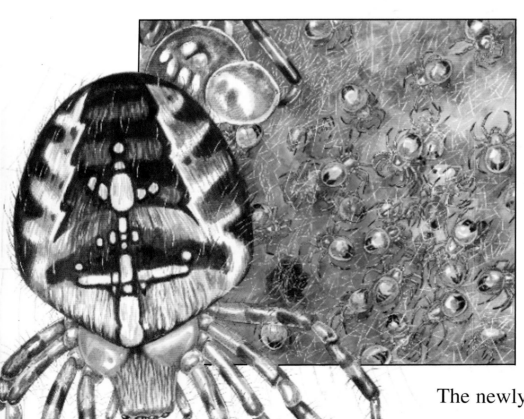

Spiderlings hatching together

The newly hatched spiderlings look like tiny versions of their mother.

## True or False?
Female spiders often eat their babies.

Answers on page 31

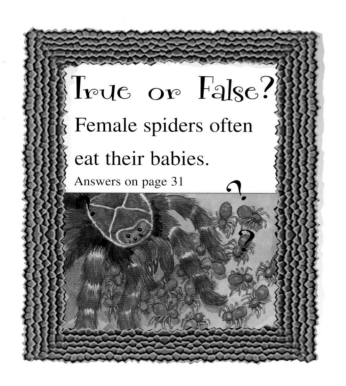

Some spiders lay their eggs in a protective silk sac.

## Spiderlings

Some mothers carry their eggs on their backs.

Wolf spiders carry their eggs in a silk sac attached to their abdomen.

## Wolf spider

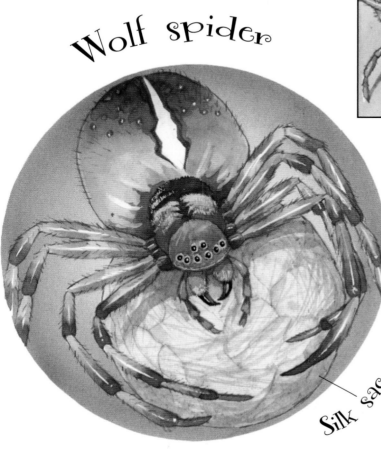

Silk sac

# How do spiders catch their prey?

**M**ost spiders catch prey using webs made from strong and sticky silk. The sticky threads trap any insects that accidently fly into the web.

Other spiders hunt in different ways – by ambushing animals or chasing them.

## How does a spider make a web?

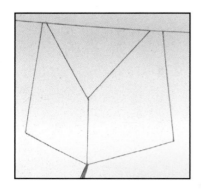

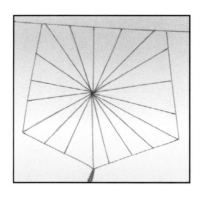

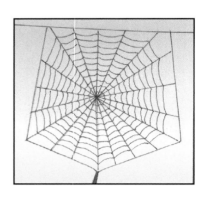

1. First the spider builds a frame with strands of silk.

2. Then it adds extra lines to strengthen the web.

3. Finally, a spiral of sticky silk thread is added to catch prey.

Silk

**True or False?**
Spiders lived before
the first dinosaurs.

? ?

Answers on page 31

When a spider catches a fly, it wraps
it in silk. Then it injects the fly with
**venom**. The venom turns the body
into liquid. The spider sucks
up this liquid.

27

# Do beetles wear armour?

Like all insects, beetles do not have a skeleton inside their body. Instead they have one on the outside, called an **exoskeleton**. This acts like a suit of armour, protecting the beetles from predators.

## Crescent-horned dung beetle

**True or False?**

Beetles can live underwater. **?**

Answers on page 31

The crescent-horned dung beetle feeds on the dung of other animals. Males use their large horn in fights with other males over **mates** and food.

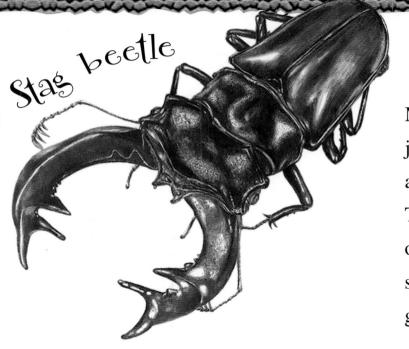

Stag beetle

Male stag beetles have big jaws that look a bit like the antlers of a stag (male deer). These help when wrestling other males. Females use their smaller jaws to dig holes in the ground and bury their eggs.

Scientists think there are around 5 million species of beetle on Earth. They range from just 0.25 mm long to a huge 19 cm.

Tiny false scorpions use the harlequin beetle to travel long distances – by hitching a ride on the beetle's back! When the beetle lands, the false scorpion jumps off.

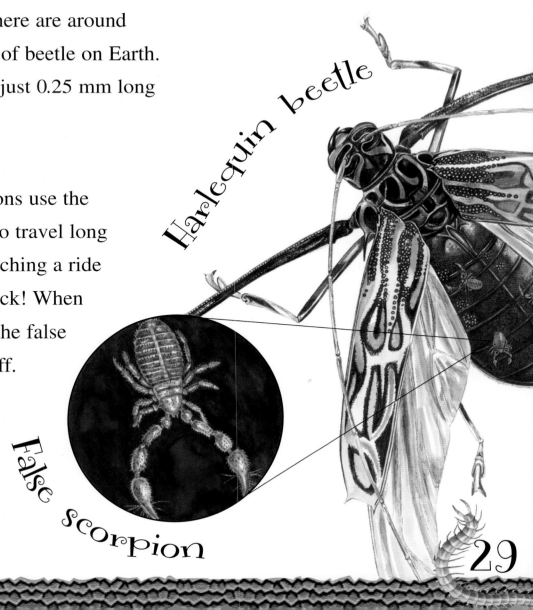

Harlequin beetle

False scorpion

# Glossary

**Abdomen**  The rear, and biggest, part of an insect's body.

**Camouflage**  Colouring or covering that makes something look like its surroundings.

**Colony**  A large group of the same type of animal that lives together.

**Exoskeleton**  The hard, outer armour of an insect's body that supports and protects its insides.

**Insect**  An invertebrate with six legs and a body made of three parts: head, thorax and adbomen.

**Invertebrate**  An animal with no backbone.

**Larvae**  The plural of **larva**: a stage in an insect's life between hatching and becoming an adult.

**Mate**  (noun) A partner of the opposite sex; (verb) to join together to make offspring.

**Nectar**  A sweet substance in flowers that butterflies and some other insects drink.

**Nocturnal**  Active mostly at night.

**Parasite**  A small creature that lives on a larger creature or feeds from it.

**Predator**  An animal that hunts another animals for food.

**Prey**  Animals that are killed and eaten by other animals.

**Queen**  The only female that can breed in a colony of ants, bees or termites.

**Social insects**  Insects that live together in large colonies.

**Species**  A group of animals that look the same, live in the same way and produce young that do the same.

**Swarm**  A large group of animals moving in the same direction.

**Thorax**  The middle part of an insect's body.

**Venom**  A form of poison.

# Answers

**Page 6 TRUE!** The larvae of weaver ants produce a sticky silk that the ants use to make nests. Worker weaver ants squeeze the larvae so that they ooze enough silk.

**Page 8 TRUE!** Although most praying mantises live on a diet of smaller insects, some will occasionally attack frogs and small rodents.

**Page 13 TRUE!** Mosquito larvae live in pools of still water. They cling to the surface from under the water, and use a tiny airway, or 'snorkel', to breathe.

**Page 14 FALSE!** Butterflies are born as caterpillars, so they don't have wings. When caterpillars are big enough, they form a hard casing called a pupa around their bodies. When they emerge from the pupa, they are butterflies – with colourful wings!

**Page 18 TRUE!** Millipedes roll up into a tight ball when disturbed by predators. Curled up like this, their soft underbelly and legs are protected by their tough armour.

**Page 23 FALSE!** Yellow crazy ants are a threat to red crabs, not the other way around. Swarms of yellow crazy ants have killed thousands of red crabs on Christmas Island, Australia, since they were introduced there 80 years ago.

**Page 25 FALSE!** Often, female spiders eat their male mates (not their babies) after mating.

**Page 27 TRUE!** Spiders lived at least 180 million years before the first dinosaurs.

**Page 28 TRUE!** The great diving beetle lives in freshwater ponds or slow-moving streams. It feeds on tadpoles, insects and small fish.

Funnel–web spider

31

# Index

(Illustrations are shown in **bold type**.)

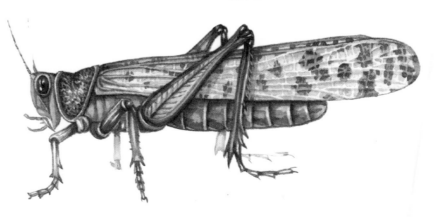
Wasp

Locust

# MINIBEASTS

Take a close look at some of Earth's most fascinating creepy-crawlies and find out how they live, hunt and breed.

Lift the special acetate pages and come face to face with some of the most unforgettable sights the insect world has to offer.

Bursting with stunning illustrations, the World of Wonder series spans a wide range of life science topics. Lively text and captions are linked to pictures to help early readers' language skills. Questions prompt discussion about how, why, what, when, and where things happen.

Titles:
- Dinosaurs
- Ocean Life
- Living World
- People and Places
- Rainforest Animals
- Earth and the Universe
- Machines and Inventions
- Prehistoric Animals

PAPER FROM SUSTAINABLE FORESTS

BOOK HOUSE

ISBN 978-1-907184-05-5

£5.99

9 781907 184055 >

www.book-house.co.uk

KNOWLEDGE IS POWER